Ortho Easy-Step Books

Landscape Design

*Created and designed
by the editorial staff of
Ortho Books*

Contents

Anyone can learn to design a new landscape or improve an existing one. A successful landscape does what you want it to, and knowing what you want is the best place to start. This book will help you discover what you would like in your yard and how to make that a reality. The basic design principles that you will need are covered. You will learn how to develop a working plan for the landscape, beginning with measuring your lot and house. From there, you will see how to draw to scale and make a base plan. Then you can "try out" different ways you would like to use your yard—this is the basis for the concept plan. Choosing plants and materials carefully is another important part of garden design. Two chapters in this book give guidelines for proper selection. After that, you will be able to make working drawings and begin the process of installing your new landscape.

Play area
(wood chips)

Service
area
(concrete)

Lawn

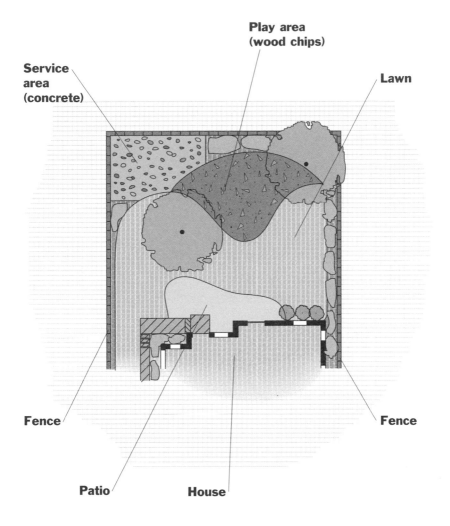

Fence

Fence

Patio

House

Planning the Landscap

1

Look at your present yard

Begin planning by looking at the landscape you already have. Study the yard from the street and the rear of the property as well as from inside the house. Make a list of what you like, such as the sun exposure different areas get over the course of the day, the flowers or fruit on existing plants, or the view in winter when the trees are bare. Also list things you don't like, such as lack of privacy, a messy tree, or too much wind. Take careful notes so you don't end up removing any of the yard's positive features.

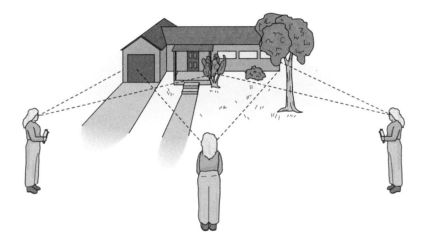

Consider your lifestyle

When planning and designing your yard, consider the function of the landscape and how well it currently satisfies your interests and needs—or how it could in the future. Plan the outdoor living areas as if they were rooms of your house. A patio off the kitchen might be designed for outdoor eating. A children's outdoor play area can be like a child's room, with ample toy storage that is low and easy to access. Landscaping tastes are personal, so consider your lifestyle carefully as you design your yard.

An Outdoor Floor Plan

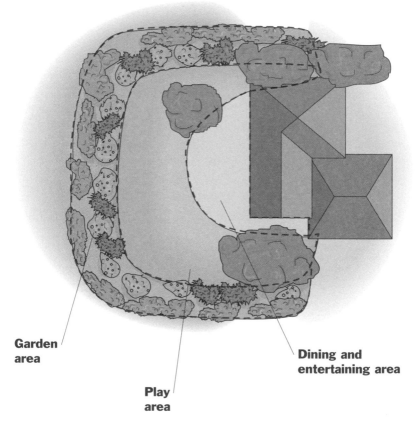

Garden
area

Play
area

Dining and
entertaining area

Ask yourself and other family members what purposes the landscape should serve, including: Who will use the yard, and how will they use it? Do we like to entertain outdoors? Do we want a cut-flower or vegetable garden? How about a protected area for sunbathing or a spa? And what about a dog run and kennel? In some landscape designs, a single function is featured, but most provide spaces for a variety of activities that appeal to the various interests of all family members.

Possible Uses of the Landscape

Outdoor Living Areas

Patio or deck

Outdoor eating area

Outdoor cooking area

Private garden

Secluded reading nook

Sunbathing area

Vantage point

Children's Play Areas

Sandbox

Lawn

Playhouse

Tree house

Swing set/climbing structure

Wading pool

Racetrack for tricycles

Platform

Recreation Areas

Game court: Tennis, basketball, handball, horseshoes, volleyball

Game lawn: Croquet, putting green, lawn bowling

Exercise circuit

Swimming pool

Spa or hot tub

Utility Areas

Garbage cans

Dog run or doghouse

Firewood storage

RV or boat storage

Storage shed

Potting shed

Composting area

Extra parking

Specialty Gardens

Vegetable garden

Cut-flower garden

Herb garden

Garden pool

Rock garden

Gather creative ideas

Look at different landscapes in your area, and those you visit elsewhere, and see which ones you like. Look at the overall scheme as well as the details. Make quick sketches or take pictures to help you remember. Note the design of the constructed elements, plant selection and groupings, and the way the landscape is laid out. Collect photographs, plans, and examples of plant combinations and design ideas from books and magazines. Put them into a file or notebook.

Review landscape styles

The most successful landscape design reflects the style and character of the home it surrounds, the physical attributes of the site, and the lives of the people who will use it. With this in mind, determine which landscape style is most suitable. Is it clean and orderly, with straight lines and neat walkways? Does it have masses of flowers like an English country garden? Perhaps you prefer the simplicity of water, rocks, and greenery as in a Japanese garden. You can combine different styles, but it generally looks better to use one style throughout.

Formal

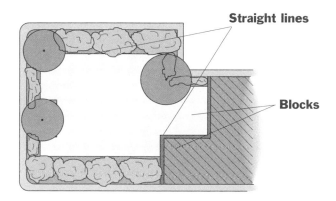

Straight lines

Blocks

Informal

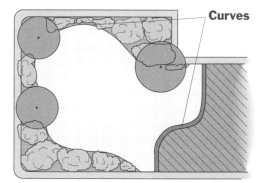

Curves

Use design concepts

The basic elements of design work together to make an attractive landscape. These include scale and proportion, repetition, balance, color, and texture. For example, large plants should not be used in a small area, because their size will be overwhelming, or out of scale. Likewise, small plants can seem lost around a large covered patio. Tall trees may be needed for a two-story house, but would overpower a one-story home. The mature size of plants should be in proportion to the house, patio, deck, or lawn area in which they are planted.

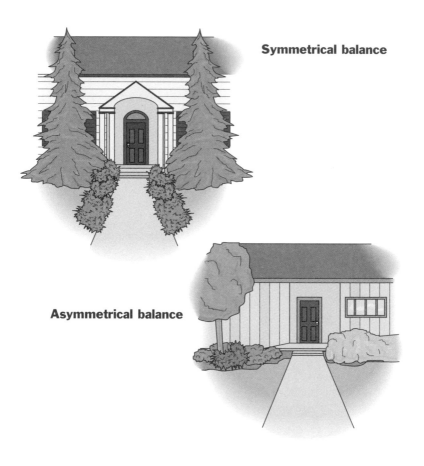

Symmetrical balance

Asymmetrical balance

Repeat similar shapes, colors, and textures to give the landscape a feeling of unity—but don't overdo it. Repeat various colors or similar types of plants throughout the entire garden, rather than just in small areas. A landscape does not need to be symmetrical to be in balance. For example, a large tree on one side of the yard can be balanced by a group of shrubs on the other side. An interesting design effect is also achieved by grouping plants of similar textures with plants of a different texture.

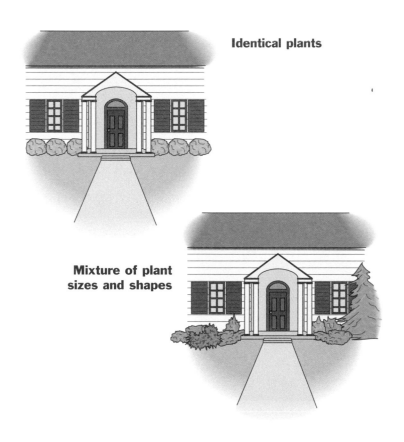

Identical plants

Mixture of plant sizes and shapes

Think about maintenance

Keep in mind the amount of effort necessary for upkeep as you design the landscape. Lawns, cut-flower and vegetable gardens, and specially trained or pruned shrubs or hedges usually take the most time to maintain properly. If you don't get consistent rainfall, install a sprinkler system (with a timer) to save you many hours of work. Buy durable construction materials that will last. Prepare the soil well and select and place plants carefully so they will need less care as they mature. Set up a convenient storage area for maintenance equipment.

Planning for Easy Maintenance

To keep your maintenance time and costs low, follow these pointers:

Keep the lawn small
Because of mowing, lawns take more maintenance time than any other type of planting. They also require lots of water. Low ground covers or mixed plantings are attractive and take less time and resources.

Put deep ground covers under messy trees
The time-consuming task of raking fallen leaves can be avoided if the leaves sift into a deep ground cover, such as ivy. There they become mulch, eventually providing nutrients to the trees and ground cover.

Select plants that don't need much work
Some plants need regular spraying, staking, pruning, and extra care. Most plants native to the area, or to an area with a similar climate, grow as though they were wild, with little attention from you. As you select plants, ask the nursery staff about the care the plants will need.

Keep the design informal
Landscape features with soft edges and uneven surfaces need less care than formal ones. For example, informal hedges can be pruned once or twice a year, but formal hedges with flat surfaces and sharp corners begin to look ragged just a few weeks after shearing. The more the landscape resembles natural scenery, the less you will have to do to keep it looking presentable.

Automate the watering
If you live in an area where you need to water regularly, install automatic irrigation. A drip emitter system or sprinkler system with a timer will save many hours of work during dry periods.

Consider the soil type

Know your soil before beginning the design process. The best soil for planting drains well, is soft and fairly easy to dig, and is free of rocks, sticks, building material, and weed seeds. It is usually dark colored and resembles cake crumbs. In soil of the proper texture, a moist clod should mold into your hand—yet crumble apart when squeezed. It should not be sticky. If you feel it would be helpful, have your soil tested at an agricultural laboratory to find out its type, nutrient content, and pH (the level of acidity or alkalinity).

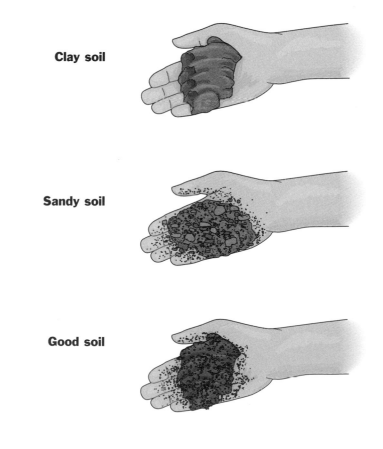

Clay soil

Sandy soil

Good soil

Find the property lines

Draw an accurate outline of your lot on drafting paper, or trace the outline from an original blueprint or plat plan (found with the deed to your home or at the local building department). To locate the property line yourself, look for markers left by surveyors on the corners of the property, such as a line in the front curb or an iron pipe driven into the ground. Often the apparent property lines such as a hedge, lawn edge, or fence are not the legal property lines, so you may want to consult a surveyor to verify them.

Plot plan

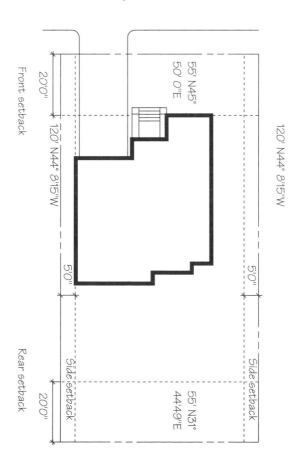

Measure the site

Using a long tape measure, begin measuring from a baseline such as a wall of the house or the front curb. Measure distances needed to locate property lines, house walls, the driveway and road, paths, fences, overhead and underground utility lines, easements and setbacks, irrigation systems, other structures, and existing shrubs and trees (along with their trunk and crown diameters). Jot down the measurements as you go. Accuracy counts more than neatness at this point.

Checklist for Measuring the Site

Check this list to make sure you don't leave anything out of the base plan.

Water meter

Site where main water line enters the house (usually in line with the meter)

Main shutoff valve

Each side of doors and windows

Height of windowsills above ground

Telephone and power lines

Electric meter

Downspouts

Clothes-dryer vent

Outdoor lights

Hose bibbs (water faucets)

Lampposts

Telephone poles

Fences and walls, with gates

All other structures

Driveway

Trees (identify species if possible)

    Trunk diameter

    Crown diameter

    Height of lowest branch

    Height of crown

Shrubs (identify species if possible)

Rock outcroppings

Banks, cliffs, steep places

T I P : An *easement* is someone else's right of access to a section of your property.

Next, measure the house in detail. Begin at a corner and lay the tape measure along one wall. On paper, label the beginning point of the tape with the letter A. Walking alongside the house from point A, record the distance to corners, windows, doors, downspouts, meters, and hose bibbs. If the wall has a bay (an area that protrudes), measure how much it extends. Measure the remaining walls of the house in the same way.

TIP: Building codes often limit *setback*—how close to the street or property line you can build.

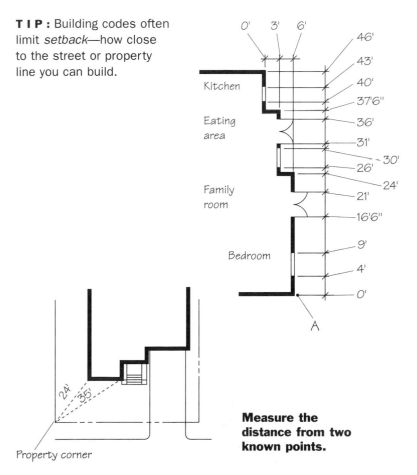

Measure the distance from two known points.

Draw to scale

After measuring and making a rough sketch, draw a more detailed plan to scale. Use a pad of graph paper lined to scale (if you choose ¼ inch to represent 1 foot, buy graph paper with ¼-inch squares). You will also need tracing paper to place over the base plan for bubble diagrams (see page 26), 45- and 60-degree triangles, a roll of drafting tape, a compass, an architect's scale, a pencil, and an eraser. Select a smooth, hard drawing surface and secure the paper with drafting tape at each corner.

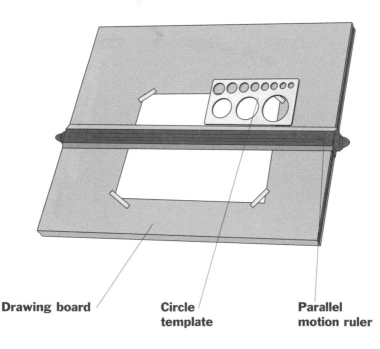

Drawing board **Circle template** **Parallel motion ruler**

Use the architect's scale to convert measured distances to the plan's scale, or count squares on the graph paper. Choose a scale that will allow the finished plan to fit comfortably on the page, such as ¼ inch equals 1 foot for a small yard, up to 1 inch equals 20 feet for a large lot. If the yard is very large, you may want to make one plan of the whole yard at a small scale first, then make separate plans for individual areas at a larger scale later.

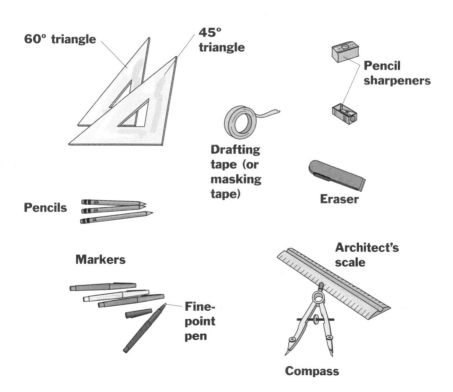

60° triangle

45° triangle

Pencil sharpeners

Drafting tape (or masking tape)

Eraser

Pencils

Markers

Fine-point pen

Architect's scale

Compass

Sketch a base plan

On a new piece of graph paper, draw the baseline from which you began measuring the site. Place the baseline carefully so you will be able to fit the entire site on the page. Using the measurements from the scale drawing, draw the house and the property lines first, then add the other major features. Measure with the scale, compass, or ruler and make dots on the plan. Join the dots for completed lines.

Mark the locations of trees and shrubs that you plan to keep by drawing a small circle to represent the trunk and a large circle to show the top. Make several photocopies or blueprints of the completed base plan for yourself and any contractors. You will be using this base plan as the basis for several more steps in the design process. Make sure the pencil marks are dark enough to show up on copies. Put the original base plan in a safe place.

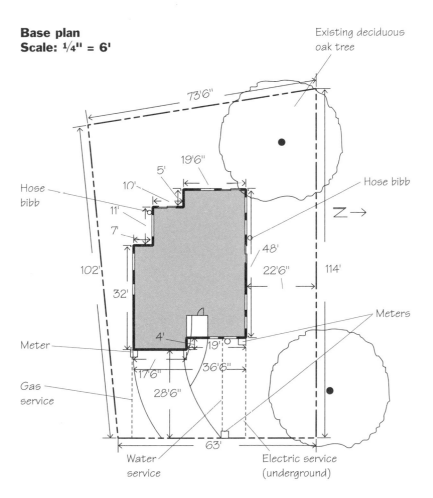

Base plan
Scale: ¼" = 6'

Existing deciduous oak tree

73'6"

19'6"

5'

10'

Hose bibb

Hose bibb

11'

7'

Z →

48'

102'

22'6"

114'

32'

Meters

Meter

4'

19'

Gas service

17'6"

36'6"

28'6"

63'

Water service

Electric service (underground)

5

Conduct a site analysis

Before moving on, take a close look at the property. Think again about what you like and don't like, and try to foresee problems. Walk around, taking notes on a copy of the base plan or on a piece of tracing paper laid over it. Indicate any feature that might affect your landscape decisions, such as wind, sun, shade, views (good and bad), slopes, or privacy needs. Make notes about neighboring properties that may be relevant, such as noise, drainage problems, or nearby trees.

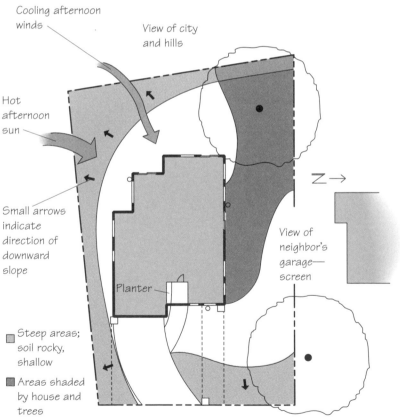

Cooling afternoon winds

View of city and hills

Hot afternoon sun

Small arrows indicate direction of downward slope

N →

View of neighbor's garage— screen

Planter

Steep areas; soil rocky, shallow

Areas shaded by house and trees

View of neighborhood

If you are renovating an existing landscape, think about what you're going to keep and what will be removed. Be cautious—if you take something out at the beginning of the project, you can't bring it back later. Large trees are usually valuable assets and worth keeping if at all possible. To make sure you fully analyze your lot, go inside and view the yard from the rooms where you spend the most time, as well as from the entryways. Note the pluses and minuses of each view. Write down everything of importance.

Site Analysis Checklist

TOPOGRAPHY
- Existing topography
- Mark the tops and bottoms of slopes
- Degree of slope: severe, moderate, minor
- Elevation of any major features, if necessary

DRAINAGE AND SOIL
- Directions of drainage with high and low spots
- Topsoil—pH
- Depth of soil

BOUNDARIES
- Property lines
- Easements—buildings, roads, etc.
- Rights-of-way

LEGAL REGULATIONS
- Zoning restrictions—setback requirements, etc.
- Building codes (check with local authorities)

EXISTING VEGETATION
- Location of all existing trees, size (height and crown), good or bad condition
- Location of shrubs and smaller plants, size (height and spread), good or bad condition

UTILITIES
- Location of all utility connections and alignments

VISUAL SURVEY
- Best views, poor views, objectionable views
- Off-site nuisance, noise, smells, etc.
- Other particular natural features, e.g., springs, sunken areas, special plants, etc.
- Orientation to sun, wind
- Existing driveway, buildings
- Problem spots
- Interior arrangement of house

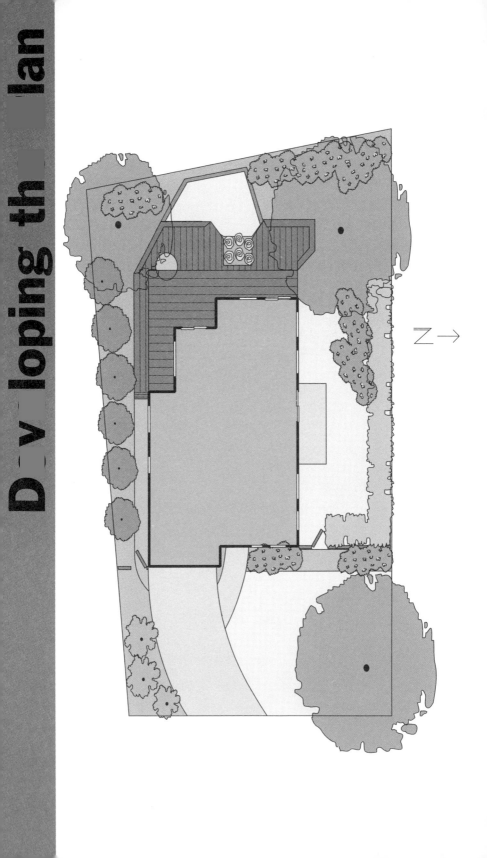

N →

Draw bubble diagrams

Do not begin the actual design process by sketching specific details on the original base plan. Instead, lay tracing paper over it and start drawing "bubbles"—rough circles that represent functional areas without defining their form. The different sizes of bubbles indicate the respective uses and relative importance of the potential areas you envision for the yard. These might include such things as an entryway, lawn, outdoor living space, vegetable garden, and service area.

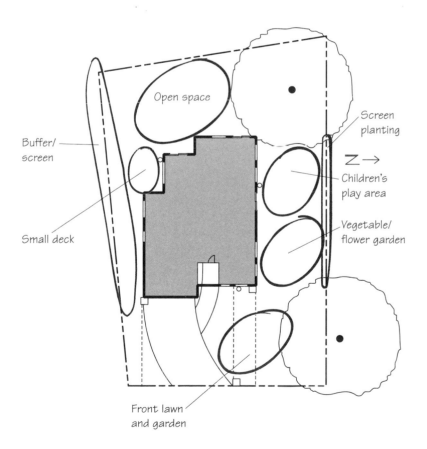

Open space

Screen planting

Buffer/ screen

Z →

Children's play area

Vegetable/ flower garden

Small deck

Front lawn and garden

2 Keep the ideas flowing

As you experiment with bubble diagrams, think about such things as views, sun/shade patterns, wind direction, and connections among the various spaces. Use arrows to show traffic flow, keeping frequently used routes as short as possible. If the arrows are too long, try a different arrangement to make access more convenient. Cut out smaller bubbles from heavier paper to represent patios, decks, or pools. Move these patterns around, using various configurations within the broader space you've allotted to that general use.

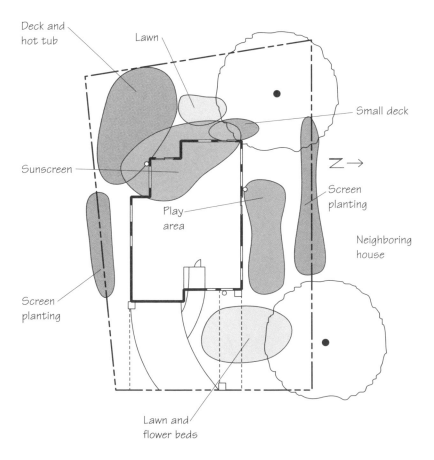

Deck and hot tub

Lawn

Small deck

Sunscreen

N →

Play area

Screen planting

Neighboring house

Screen planting

Lawn and flower beds

Double-check all dimensions to ensure that all the elements fit. Refer to your list of all the things you would like to do in the yard. Get feedback on your bubble diagrams from family members or any others who you feel can assist you. Once several agreeable combinations have been developed, go back over each one and see whether it accomplishes the design goals. Choose the one you like best. This will be the basis for the concept plan.

Design Checklist

Once the base plan has been completed, including all the necessary notes, ask yourself the following questions. This will help ensure that the design you come up with is workable.

Uses of the Yard

Which of the present uses of the yard are important to preserve and which should be eliminated?

What are the functions of the redesigned landscape? Think about how the landscape will incorporate the right amount of space and equipment for such things as relaxing, entertaining, recreation, children's play, vegetable and flower gardening, keeping pets, and other activities.

Elements of the New Design

Is there a particular landscape style you want to follow?

Should some areas be more private or more accessible?

What outdoor rooms do you want to create in the new landscape? What are their purposes?

Are there any plants, structures, or other elements you want to add?

Practical Considerations and Special Needs

Will the plans affect neighbors? If so, have you discussed this with them?

What is the budget for the project? Can the project be done in stages to fit within the budget and still fulfill your long-term plans?

Are the materials for the project readily available and affordable?

How much time do you have to carry out planning, design, and installation?

Do you have the necessary tools, skills, and patience to complete the project yourself?

Will you have time to maintain the landscape once it is installed?

Are any members of the family allergic to bee stings or certain plants?

Do you need to allow for wheelchair access?

Have you thought about water conservation?

Do you want to attract birds and other wildlife?

Sketch a concept plan

Draw a concept plan from your favorite bubble diagram. This will help define how the spaces in the landscape might actually look. For example, an area marked for "play" on the bubble diagram might be defined as a lawn twice as long as it is wide, and separated from other areas by a line of shrubs. The "outdoor eating area" might become a brick patio connected to the kitchen by a path. When determining the size to make the spaces, use as a guide the proportions of the equivalent indoor room.

Three Types of Sketches

Bird's-eye view

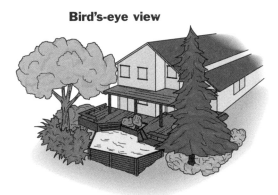

Elevation   **Section**

A space intended for outdoor grilling and dining can, as a starting point, follow the dimensions of the existing kitchen and eating area. But do not make outdoor spaces such as patios and decks so large that they are uncomfortable and inconvenient. If a deck or patio will be used mostly for entertaining, think of how much space it takes to entertain the same number of people indoors and whether more space will be needed outdoors. A sense of intimacy outdoors depends upon the size of the area in relation to its purpose.

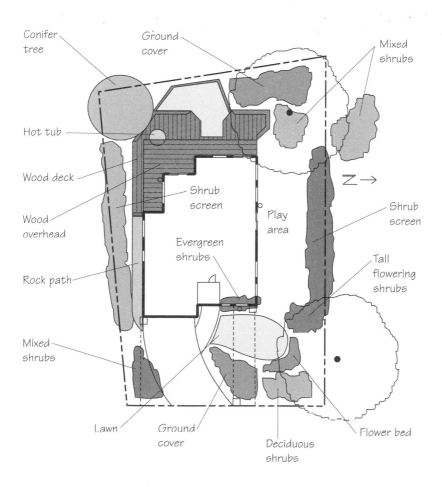

Conifer tree

Ground cover

Mixed shrubs

Hot tub

Wood deck

Shrub screen

Play area

Wood overhead

Evergreen shrubs

N→

Shrub screen

Rock path

Tall flowering shrubs

Mixed shrubs

Lawn

Ground cover

Deciduous shrubs

Flower bed

Think three-dimensionally

To get a better idea of what the landscape will look like, draw some simple elevation sketches. They needn't be completely accurate, although the greater the detail, the easier it will be to picture the results. You can also take photographs of your home, make enlarged photocopies of them, and sketch in possible ideas. To start, photograph the sites from the point from which you'll most often view them. If there are existing plants and outdoor structures, take the photos from a stepladder so you can better see over them.

House Elevation—Front Yard

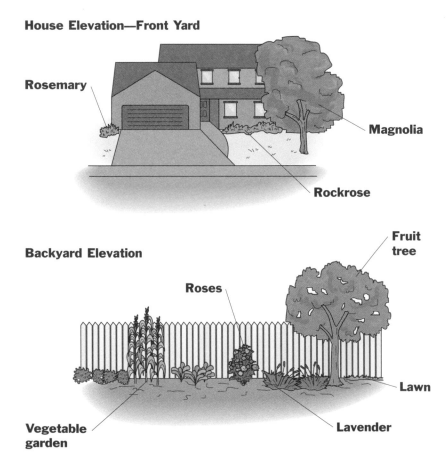

Rosemary

Magnolia

Rockrose

Backyard Elevation

Fruit tree

Roses

Lawn

Vegetable garden

Lavender

Have 4-inch by 6-inch prints made and, on a photocopier, enlarge the ones that best display the sites. If the copier has a "Photo" button, use it. Directly on the copies, or on a tracing-paper overlay, draw the major elements—the outline of the house and existing shrubs, trees, and paths that will remain. Sketch new plants at their approximate mature size, as well as planned patios, walls, fences, and so on. When you've got the design you want, go over the pencil lines in black marker so you can see them clearly.

Test the ideas outside

Go outdoors and try out your plans in the yard itself. Use a garden hose to plot the layout of walkways, patios, planting beds, ponds, and other landscape features. For a curved walkway, place on the ground pieces of wood lath cut to the same length to maintain an even width. Use brown wrapping paper (sold by the roll) to model patios, walkways, and other paved surfaces. Test different paving patterns by tracing the shapes on the paper with colored chalk.

Garden hose

Wood lath

TIP: The most direct walkway is not always the most desirable. Plan routes to provide a pleasing sequence of views.

Buy or borrow sample construction materials such as brick or interlocking concrete pavers and arrange them on-site to see which types look best. Use wood stakes or potted plants to get an idea of how planted areas will look. Return to your vantage point to check the results; make changes until you are satisfied. While testing your ideas, look at the landscape from downstairs and upstairs windows, from the front sidewalk and the street, and from neighboring yards. Consider how time of day and seasonal changes will affect sun/shade patterns in the yard.

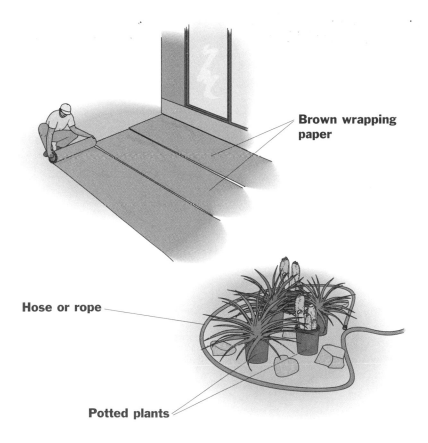

Brown wrapping paper

Hose or rope

Potted plants

1

Select walls

There are two types of landscape walls: freestanding and retaining. Use walls to define outdoor areas, increase the amount of level yard, stop soil erosion, and improve the appearance of the home and garden. Make them with reinforced concrete, timber, or dry-laid or mortared stone. When choosing materials, consider style, cost, ease of installation, and durability. Wherever possible, limit the height of landscape walls to 3 feet, as local building codes usually require deep concrete footings and specific construction techniques for taller ones.

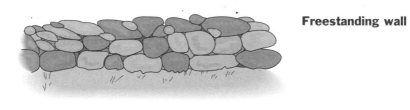

Freestanding wall

Retaining wall

Utilize fences

Fences frame, accent, provide protection and privacy, and can form a background to set off plantings. Choose a style, color, and form that will unify the yard and home. If desired, you can mix opaque and open styles to cover unsightly views but frame and heighten pleasant ones. Fences can be tall for privacy or short for accent. You can cover fences with vines or espaliers (plants trained along a support system in a specific design or form) for vertical gardening and perhaps a softening as well as sound-deadening effect.

Picket fence

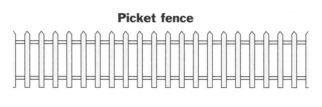

Rail fence

Grape stake fence

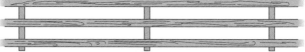

Basket-weave fence

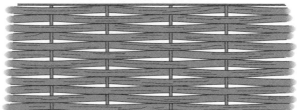

Plan for walkways

Make walkways of brick, flagstone, woodblocks, pavers, or cobblestone—all of which are usually set in sand. Solid concrete, exposed aggregate, pebbles, gravel, pine needles, wood chips, or ground bark can also be used. Choose materials that complement the house and yard. Walks should follow the natural flow of traffic and be comfortable and safe. In entry and service areas, make them solid and definite; elsewhere, they can be more casual. Make walks at least 3 feet wide—wider at curves and ends. Keep back plants or structures alongside.

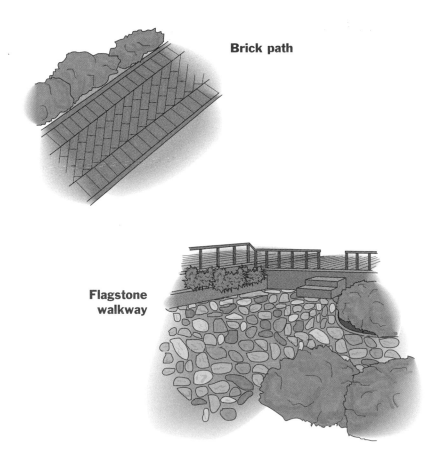

Brick path

Flagstone walkway

Provide steps

Made of wood, concrete, or rustic materials such as split logs, landscape timbers, or rough-cut stone, steps should be in harmony with the surrounding area. Make them as broad as the path that leads to them and less steep than stairs used indoors. Ramp steps are a series of single steps alternating with sloping surfaces. For slight grade changes, leave the slope as it is rather than build a step. For better drainage, angle the step tread forward slightly. Use a railing on at least one side for safety and where codes require it.

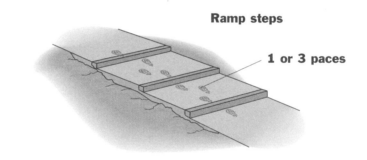

Ramp steps

1 or 3 paces

**Recessed steps
(blend with slope)**

Protruding steps

Consider a deck

Use decks to gain outdoor living space on level, sloping, or hilly lots. They work best when connected to a kitchen, family room, or dining room. They can be built around existing trees without changing the ground level. With various railings and trellises, decks can be made to fit into either natural or formal settings. A deck is more interesting and attractive if at least one corner is rounded or angled, the pattern or the levels are varied, and it is surrounded with complementary planters or plantings.

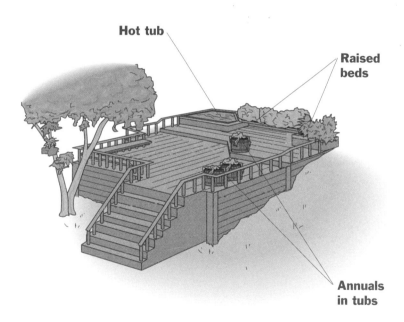

Hot tub

Raised beds

Annuals in tubs

Enjoy a patio

Pave patios with brick, tile, flagstone, wood, pavers, cobblestone, solid concrete, or exposed aggregate. Connected to the family room, dining room, or kitchen, they serve well as outdoor eating or entertaining areas. In front of a home, they can serve as a porch or courtyard. A patio will also make a narrow side yard more usable. Consider sun/shade patterns and wind direction when locating patios. Be sure the drainage under them is adequate. Consider using plants or railings for privacy, and arbors or roofs for shade.

Plan for irrigation

Consult a sprinkler dealer to determine the layout, equipment, and type of watering system (drip emitter and/or sprinklers) that will work best for you. Bring a detailed site plan that identifies the types of plants and the soil conditions, along with the water pressure at your house in gallons per minute. This can be measured with a simple gauge that screws onto a hose bibb; or you can measure how long it takes to fill a 1- or 5-gallon container with the pressure on full force.

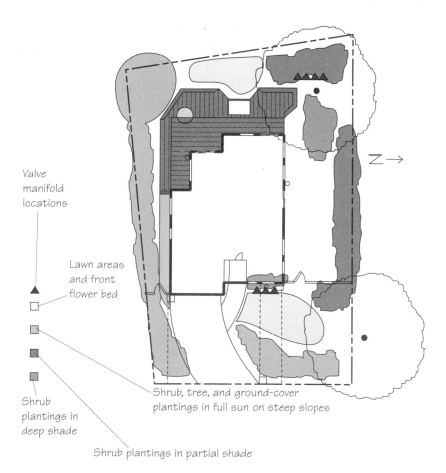

Valve
manifold
locations

Lawn areas
and front
flower bed

Shrub
plantings in
deep shade

Shrub, tree, and ground-cover
plantings in full sun on steep slopes

Shrub plantings in partial shade

N →

Make sensible choices

Select plants adapted to the climate and to the various soil and sun conditions in your garden. If the location receives hot afternoon sun or is shaded, if it drains poorly or has sandy soil, select plantings that tolerate those conditions. Choose plants with their mature size in mind, and give them room to grow. Be aware of potential problems, such as trees with weak crotches that break in storms, shallow roots that can push up sidewalks, or fruit that drops to stain the surface below.

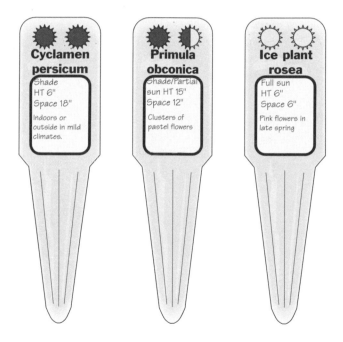

Cyclamen persicum
Shade
HT 6"
Space 18"

Indoors or outside in mild climates.

Primula obconica
Shade/Partial sun HT 15"
Space 12"

Clusters of pastel flowers

Ice plant rosea
Full sun
HT 6"
Space 6"

Pink flowers in late spring

Choose shade trees

Besides filtering or blocking the sun, shade trees provide framing, privacy, and vertical or skyline interest to the landscape. They tie a house to its site and provide protection from the elements. Trees that shed their leaves let in the winter sun to brighten and warm the area. Plant one or two of the largest trees you can afford. If need be, use quick-growing ones until other, choicer selections grow enough for the desired effect. Examples of shade trees include ash, cork oak, ginkgo, goldenrain tree, honeylocust, magnolia, maple, oak, and tulip tree.

Summer   **Winter**

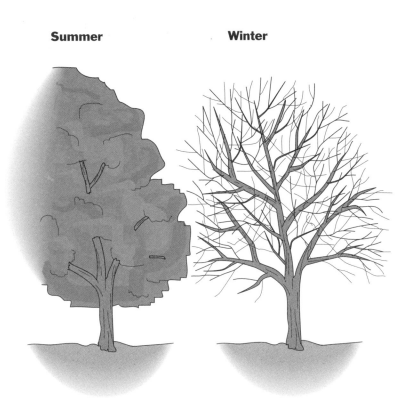

T I P : If a tree will exceed 20 feet high when mature, plant it at least 15 feet from the house.

Position accent trees

Accent (also known as specimen or ornamental) trees create interest or a focal point in a landscape. Place them where they can be clearly seen from indoors, the street, or the entrance. Keep fruit trees away from the driveway or patio because of their debris. Accent trees work well against a house, fence, or evergreen background. When choosing them, consider their mature size and scale relative to the house. Apple, birch, cherry, cherry-laurel, crab apple, dogwood, hawthorn, holly, Japanese maple, and redbud are types of accent trees.

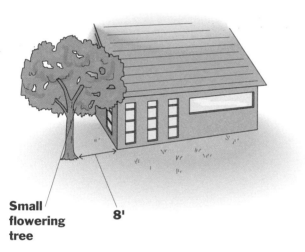

Small flowering tree   **8'**

T I P : For foundation plantings, allow three feet between the house and trunks for most shrubs; give junipers four feet.

4

Decide on shrub varieties

Shrubs and bushes are medium-sized woody plants that are often used between large structures or trees and low-growing flowers or lawns.

Planted individually or in groups, they provide color and shape and usually require little care. Deciduous shrubs lose their leaves in the late fall or winter, whereas evergreens retain their leaves year-round. Accent or specimen shrubs can be used as focal points, because they offer something striking such as flowers or fruit, seasonal color, general form, or winter foliage.

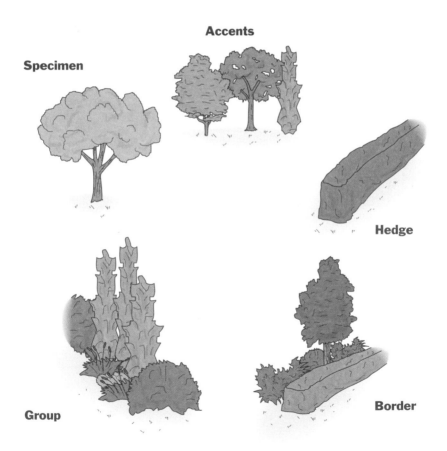

Accents

Specimen

Hedge

Group

Border

5

Use hedges and screens

Many shrubs make fine screens because they grow quickly. A single plant will provide enough privacy for some areas—a side window or front door, for instance. Other areas may need a group of plants. Make the grouping all the same, or carefully mix varieties. Choose sizes that will not overgrow their space. Clipped types of hedge or screening plants include barberry, eugenia, hazelnut, juniper, privet, and yew. Unclipped varieties include arborvitae, boxwood, currant, elderberry, quince, and roses.

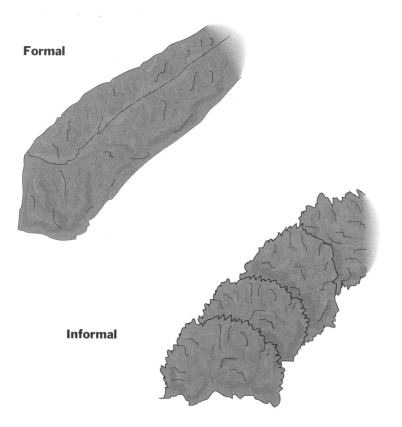

Formal

Informal

Select a lawn type

Lawns give a clean, attractive look to a yard and provide a living surface that will withstand more traffic than any other plant. Few yards would be complete without at least some areas of green grass. Lawns look best when bordered with informal groups of trees or perennial flowers that create a natural, meadow-like look. Most grass types require several hours of sun a day, as well as quite a bit of time, water, and work—more so than other plants. So don't seed or sod more grass than you want to mow or irrigate.

Types of Lawn Grass

Cool-season grasses	Warm-season grasses
■ Adapted to northern regions	■ Adapted to southern regions
■ Stay green in mild climates	■ Turn brown in cold weather
■ Suffer during hot weather	■ Thrive in hot weather
Bluegrass	Bermudagrass
Tall fescue	Bahiagrass
Fine fescue	Centipedegrass
Ryegrass	St. Augustine grass
Bentgrass	Zoysiagrass

Choose ground covers

Ground covers will grow almost anywhere: in narrow areas, on steep slopes, under trees where it is too shady for grass, or in large areas that receive full sun. They offer interesting textures, colors, and blooms. You can choose from ones that are only a few inches high to those that grow several feet tall. Ground covers can be annual or perennial, evergreen or deciduous, or for shade or sun. Examples include arisia, baby's tears, bugleweed, cotoneaster, gazania, hypericum, ivy, junipers, pachysandra, rosemary, and ornamental strawberry.

Spacing Guide for Ground Covers

Inches between plants	Square feet 64 plants will cover	Square feet 100 plants will cover
4	7	11
6	16	26
8	28	44
10	45	70
12	64	100
15	100	156
18	144	225
24	256	400

Formulas to determine square feet:

Circles: Area = diameter squared × 0.7854

Triangles: Area = $\frac{1}{2}$ base × height

Rectangles: Area = base × height

Use flowers for color

Many plants produce showy flowers, including a number of ground covers, vines, shrubs, and trees. Annuals (plants living for one year or less) and perennials (those growing several years and spreading from the same roots each year) are best known for their flowers. Available in hundreds of species and well suited for informal flower beds, formal garden arrangements, and for planting in containers, annuals such as pansies, petunias, and marigolds provide bright color throughout the year, but must be planted each year.

Meadowlike planting

Perennials such as phlox, daisies, chrysanthemums, and penstemons form the basis of many flower borders because they come up every year and require minimal care. For greatest appeal, combine perennials with their height, color, and time of bloom in mind. Many will bloom again if pruned back after they flower. Like annuals, perennials can also be used in containers and hanging baskets, both of which can be moved if necessary. Be sure to use well-draining soil in containers, and water as often as needed to keep the soil from drying out.

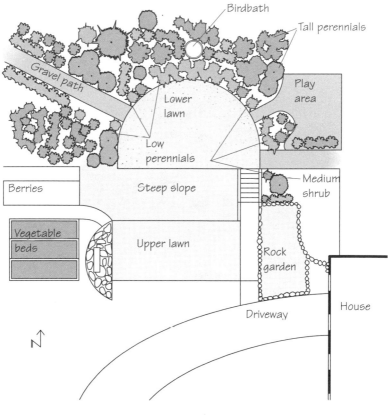

Scale ¹/₁₆" = 1'

Use drafting symbols

Specific drafting symbols are used in landscape drawings to show plants and structures. Draw symbols to scale, as close as possible to the plants' mature size. They do not have to be detailed, but it is important to label them clearly. To show trees, draw a small circle or dot to represent the trunk and a larger circle to show the crown. Show what, if anything, will be planted under the canopy. If possible, connect plants of the same type with light lines to show that they are a grouping.

Deciduous tree

Evergreen tree

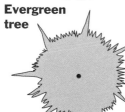

Shrub

Flowering shrub

Hedge/screen

Ground cover

Vine

Vegetables

Annuals

Gravel

Concrete

Lawn

Wood deck

Fence and gate

Draw the working plan

A working plan is an accurate, scaled rendition of the concept plan. It indicates what kind, what size, and how many of each item will be needed to complete the project. Draw your working plan neatly and concisely on a copy of the original base plan. Make sketches and any notations bold so they can be read easily and so clear copies can be made. Check that the plan includes everything and that it fits the time and budget necessary to execute it.

Preparing the Working Plan

When you're ready to commit to a working plan, ask yourself these questions:

- Does the plan meet all building codes and deed, setback, or easement requirements?
- Have I tried to solve all of the problems presented on my site analysis?
- Are my choices realistic in terms of the cost, work, and time involved to implement them?
- Will the landscape I've planned provide for all the functions my family wants, or at least the most necessary ones?
- Is the plan in keeping with our lifestyle? Does it fit my family? Will my family fit it?
- Can we safely move vehicles on and off the property and park them where needed?
- Is there easy access from the car to the kitchen or front door, from indoor rooms to outdoor living spaces, and from the garden to the shed?
- Will the yard be pleasant to the eye, ear, and nose in every season? From indoors looking out, from the street looking in, from the outdoors looking around?

If you need to, you can remain vague on the working plan about the specifics of structure design and materials. The staff at the local nursery and building-supply center can help you make decisions about specific plants and structural details after looking at your final site plan. Wherever possible, use the standard sizes of available materials. For example, if fencing boards come in 4-, 6-, and 8-foot lengths, don't decide to make a 5½-foot fence; it will waste material and create extra work and expense.

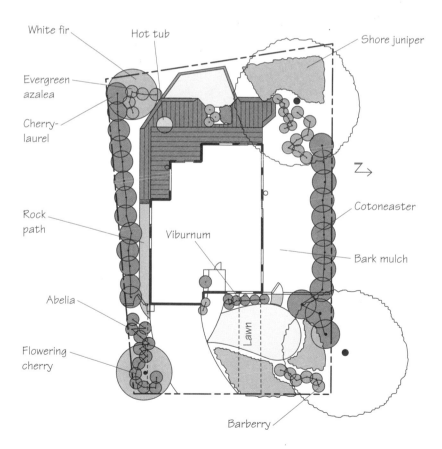

Make a cost estimate

One of the easiest ways to make a cost estimate is to list all the materials needed from each type of supplier. Put the plants, lumber, plumbing, and other materials on separate lists after having checked off every item from your working plan. When you list building materials, remember details such as nails, hardware, and paint or stain. Once these lists are complete with specific materials, quantities required, sizes and dimensions, catalog numbers, and other helpful ordering information, call or visit suppliers to find out which offer the best prices.

Remember that buying in quantity as well as purchasing from the original source of the supplies usually results in lower prices. Unless you are used to estimating costs, give yourself a contingency factor of 20 to 40 percent to compensate for overlooked items, changes in the plan, and unforeseen problems. When picking up the materials, look for any flaws in quality. Check plants for overall form, general health, and possible signs of being root bound. Before signing for a delivery, make sure it includes everything you ordered.

4

Schedule the work

First list the various tasks you foresee for the landscape project. Then, make out a schedule that specifies the order of approach and the approximate starting and completion dates for each task. Allow time to shop for materials and prepare the site before starting construction. Assign a time frame in terms of hours, days, or weeks to each task—allowing time to make mistakes and work out problems—and transfer the jobs to a calendar. Take into account the season and weather, and remember that many projects take longer than planned.

Landscaping Tasks

These are some typical tasks leading up to a finished landscape. Your job will probably not have all the same tasks, and you may not do them in exactly this order, but use this as a guide and checklist.

1. Measure the site and make a base plan.

2. Plan the landscape.

3. Clean the site.

4. Shape the ground, making the rough grade.

5. Put in drainage and irrigation systems.

6. Build terracing and retaining walls.

7. Make patios and paths.

8. Build decks, fences, and other aboveground structures.

9. Prepare the soil for plants, making the final grade.

10. Plant trees, shrubs, and hedges.

11. Plant flowers, vegetables, and ground covers.

12. Plant lawns.

Hire professionals

Using landscape professionals or qualified laborers can save time and simplify complicated jobs. Professional designers can help you plan and budget your projects, and contractors can save you time and headaches on large, difficult tasks such as grading. The abilities and reputations of designers and contractors vary greatly, so always check references and view samples of previous work before hiring. Make sure to get a written, itemized estimate, terms for payment, and proof of bonding and insurance before hiring someone to help you.

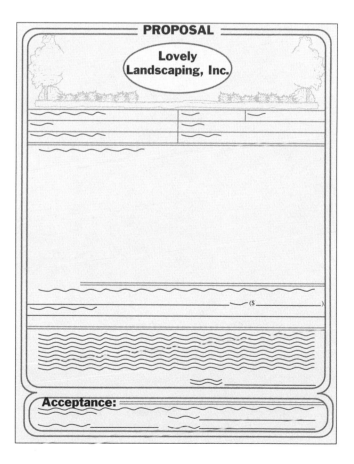

Work in stages

You may not want to carry out the whole plan immediately. Divide it into a series of manageable projects that you, or professionals you hire, can complete as time and money permit. Be sure to complete as much major grading, underground plumbing and wiring, and aboveground construction as possible before preparing the soil and planting anything. Whether you do the work over a series of weekends or years, breaking large jobs into small segments makes your goal attainable.

If the project requires digging, request an inspection and have locations of buried utility lines marked before you dig.